The Thank You BOOK

for Kids

Hundreds of Creative,
Cool, and Clever Ways to
Say Thank You!

Ali Lauren Spizman

Longstreet Press
Atlanta, Georgia

Published by
LONGSTREET PRESS
2140 Newmarket Parkway
Suite 122
Marietta, GA 30067

Printed in the United States of America

1st printing 2001

Library of Congress Catalog Card Number: 00-111984

ISBN 1-56352-640-9

Cover and book design by Jill Dible

Dedication

This book is dedicated to my
family, who taught me the true
meaning of the words "thank you,"
and to kids all over the planet,
who will help spread thank-yous
in their corners of
the world.

Thanks to Some Very Special People!

There aren't enough thanks in the world that I can express to the people who have contributed so much to my life. First of all, I would like to thank my friend and my mentor, my mom. Thanks to her guidance, my book was possible. Since I was a little girl, she has taught me that saying thank you is a way of life, and now it's my turn to thank the best mom on earth! Plus, a bigger-than-life thanks to my dad and my brother Justin for their support and love while I was writing this book. They are my best critics and are appreciated far beyond words. To my wonderful and totally grand grandparents Phyllis and Jack Freedman and Gus and Regina Spizman, who deserve a thank-you from the bottom of my heart. To Aunt Genie, Uncle Doug, Uncle Sam, Aunt Lois, Uncle Jerry, and Aunt Ramona, I am so lucky to have you all in my life! And to Bettye Storne, who brightens my every day and puts a smile on my face, and to Mary Billingsley, for her unending love. ❀ I would also like to acknowledge the amazing team at Longstreet Press, including my publisher Scott Bard, Barbara Babbit Kaufman, my editor Tysie Whitman, book designer Jill Dible, Robyn Richardson, Amy Burton, and the dedicated group of people who made this book possible. And to my fabulous friends, my endless thanks for all your support and good-luck wishes with my book. My final appreciation goes to all the individuals, from celebrities to teachers to friends and family, who added a very special thank-you touch to this book. ❀

Table of Contents

Hi there!

My name is Ali Spizman and I am 14 years old. I
wrote this book because I discovered that writing thank-
you notes and saying thank you could really be fun. It
took me a while to learn how, but when I started writing really meaningful notes I learned that each note
could be a very special gift in itself.

    Regardless of how you received this book, I want to
thank you for taking the time to read and use it. Let it
serve as a reference guide when you don't know what to
say or find yourself at a loss for words. (That happens
to all of us!)

    Saying thank you is a very powerful way to let some-
one know that you appreciate them. I believe that if
everyone took a little more time to express a thank-you,
then the world would be a kinder and sweeter place to live.

    So thanks for joining me in my thank-you mis-
sion. I hope that this book will guide you to writing
awesome thank-you notes and inspire you to be a
thank-you kid, too!

THANKS TO YOU!
Ali Spizman

What You Can Expect to See in This Book:

◎ You'll find tons of helpful examples of thank-you notes and a variety of really terrific ways that will inspire you to say thank you! Plus, fun ideas that will get you started writing thank-you notes that will mean the world to others.

◎ You'll discover creative details for decorating your stationery and designing stationery on the computer that really looks professional. Before you know it, you'll be in the thank-you business!

◎ You'll be inspired by thank-yous ranging from the edible to the incredible that will help you get your point across!

◎ You'll learn a bunch of neat tips to express your thanks and feelings for someone more creatively, including making your own gifts, using the Internet— as well as super-cool ways to express yourself through the wild and wonderful world of words.

◎ You'll find out how you can write famous people and members of your community. I'll share with you some amazing letters that I received from some amazing people who wrote me back.

SO STAY TUNED!

Thank You! Thank You!
Thank You!
THANK YOU! Thank You!
Thank You! Thank You!
Thank You!
Thank You! Thank You!
Thank You!
THANK YOU! Thank You!
THANK YOU! Thank You! Thank You!
Thank You! Thank You!
Thank You! Thank You!
Thank You! Thank You!
Thank You!
Thank You! THANK YOU! Thank You!
Thank You! Thank You!

Chapter One

Be a Thank-You Kid!

Before you think to yourself that saying thanks is silly or writing thank-you notes is a boring waste of time, look at all the amazing things a thank-you note can do.

A THANK-YOU NOTE CAN...

Make someone feel good.

Cheer a person up.

Let friends know you appreciate them.

Tell family members you love them.

Express your appreciation for a really neat gift.

Compliment someone you really care about.

Tell famous people you are proud of them.

Share your feelings of gratitude with
someone who was nice to you.

Let someone know his or her
thoughtful deed was noticed.

Explain how much someone means to you.

Encourage someone to keep up the great work.

Say what's in your heart and express it in words.

Spread really good news about you or your family.

Tell people in other cities that you are
thinking about them.

Let someone know he or she is missed.

Help you stay in touch with people you care about.

. . . .

A THANK-YOU NOTE CAN BE
A GIFT ALL BY ITSELF!

> *It's Easy to Write Thank-You Notes,*
> *and Here Is a Quick Guide to Help You Write*
> *Witty, Wise, and Wonderful Ones.*

How to Start Smart

Here are some helpful tips that will put you on the right track to saying thank you. Being prepared makes it even easier, so here are some ways to get started:

CREATE A THANK-YOU KIT. Create a letter-writing kit and fill it with stationery, envelopes, stickers, stamps, pens, and pencils. I like to use a clear plastic envelope that's big enough to hold everything. You can also use a folder or shoebox.

DECORATE YOUR STATIONERY. Personalize your stationery for a special touch. It's fun to decorate your stationery with your name and all kinds of designs. I make my own stationery on the computer with my name in all types of funky styles. It's fun to design stationery and it's a perfect activity, especially when you're bored or have nothing to do. I also like to make my own personalized address labels. You can transform ordinary paper into works of art with stickers, colorful designs, magic markers, and crayons.

Clever Tips for Making Your Own Thank-You Cards, Gifts, and Stationery:

RECYCLE GREETING CARDS. All you have to do is cover up the writing inside and it's just like new. You can also make thank-you frames for photographs by cutting out a section on the front of the card and taping a photograph of you underneath so it shows through. The front of the card will be a picture frame and you can write your message inside.

A ROUND OF THANKS. Paper plates make fun thank-you notes. Try writing a thank-you note in a circular fashion around a small, white, uncoated paper plate. You can then trim it by punching holes around the edges and lacing them with yarn or ribbon. Talk about creative!

BE ORIGINAL. Make your own stationery by drawing a picture with a black marker and have it photocopied and duplicated. You can easily have your drawings made into special thank-you notes.

CREATE A WORK OF ART TO EXPRESS YOUR THANKS. Artwork can be a perfect thank-you. Draw a picture of you and the person you are thanking, or something that represents what they mean to you, like a beautiful rainbow or vase of flowers. This can be done on your thank-you note or on a separate piece of paper and included when you send your words of thanks.

These two drawings are ones I did when I was five. My mom made photocopies of them both and used them as her favorite thank-you stationery. She still uses them today!

MAKE AN ADDRESS BOOK. I write all of my addresses in an address book. I take my address book with me when I'm writing letters at camp. I make sure that I also get all of my friends' e-mail addresses so I can stay in touch.

LEARN ABOUT STAMPS. Every letter you write needs a stamp on the envelope to mail it. I love to select my own stamps, and there are so many choices. I prefer self-sticking stamps and love selecting interesting ones. You can learn a lot about stamps through collecting them. It's fun to go to your local post office and learn all about how many stamps are needed to send your letters. Also, be sure your stamp sticks to your envelope. If it falls off, your letter will come back to you or it might even get lost!

WRITE NEATLY. Hundreds of thousands of letters end up in a place at the post office called the dead-letter file. You don't want your letters to end up there because no one knows what to do with your letter! So write neatly, check your addresses, and make sure you spell the person's name correctly. Plus, don't forget to add your return address. If something happens and your letter cannot be delivered, the post office will return it right back to you like a boomerang.

Here Are the Bits & Pieces That Make a Thank-You Note Super!

WHOSE THANK-YOU NOTE IS IT? Your name and address are important details to add to every thank-you note. I like to create thank-you notes or use ones that have my name somewhere on them. Your address should be somewhere on the envelope so that someone can write you back and your mail can be returned, just in case.

BEGIN WITH A SALUTATION: A salutation is a fancy word for "Dear So and So." It's a hello that starts your thank-you note and says to whom you are writing, such as "Dear Aunt Genie" or "Greetings, Uncle Doug!"

THE MAIN CONTENT OF THE NOTE: The main part of a thank-you note is called the body. This is where you express your feelings and make it clear how you really feel.

SIGNING OFF: The closing is how you sign your letter, such as "Thanks again, Ali." Personally, I love to be clever when I'm closing a thank-you note. I like to write "Hugs and Smiles, Ali." You'll find loads of creative ways to sign a note in this book, so don't be boring!

YOUR SIGNATURE: When signing a thank-you note, it's a good idea to write neatly so everyone knows who wrote it. Pretend that you are icing a cake and this is the finishing touch.

. . . .

P.S.
Sometimes I like to add what is called a postscript in letter land. You know it better by calling it a P.S. (like "P.S. I love you" or "P.S. I miss you"). It's a great way to get an extra point across.

. . . .

P.S. IT CAN ALSO BE USED IF YOU

FORGOT AN IMPORTANT THOUGHT,

JUST LIKE THIS ONE!

A Picture-Perfect Thank-You Note

There are good thank-you notes and then really great, memorable ones that hug people's hearts. To thank someone properly, be sure to describe how you felt when you received the gift. Describe what the person gave you and be specific.

Here's an O.K. Note:

Dear Mr. and Mrs. Freedman,

Thank you for the gift. I will really enjoy using it. Thank you for thinking of me on my birthday.

Sincerely,

Jeremy

Here's a Really Memorable Note:

Dear Mr. and Mrs. Freedman,

Your gift hit a home run with me. When I first opened your present, I thought I was seeing things. How did you ever know that I collect autographed base-balls? Your gift was a perfect match, since I know every baseball legend in history. You must be a mind reader, because I've always wanted something signed by the one and only Hank Aaron.

I will always enjoy your gift. Even as I get older, it'll be one of my prized possessions.

Thanks again for your great gift,

Jeremy

Ali's Tips for Writing Thank-You Notes:

WRITE LIKE YOU TALK OR THINK! Write your note as if you were talking to the person. Have a pretend conversation with them in your mind, and then write how you feel and what you thought. None of us are born knowing how to write, but it's easy to learn.

MAKE YOUR NOTE WITTY, funny, enthusiastic, or thoughtful, just like you. By choosing words that express your feelings, you can be a magician and make a really amazing note appear right before your eyes. Show your style by writing thank-you notes that express your personality.

BE SPECIFIC. When writing a thank-you note, pretend you are a newspaper writer and give the details! Like any good reporter, your goal is to paint a picture with words. Remember, a thank-you note is a gift, too. You wouldn't want to send a boring gift!

BE SURE TO ADD ENOUGH POSTAGE and the correct stamp to your letter. Plus, check and double-check the address and your spelling.

IF YOU ARE WRITING TO THANK SOMEONE and requesting a photograph or return letter, be sure to include your name and address. A self-addressed, stamped, return envelope will also help you get a letter back

11

sooner. Plus, be patient. If you have requested a return letter, especially if you have written someone famous, remember it takes time for people to write you back. Stay cool!

Whom Are You Going to Thank? Create a Thank-You List.

Now that you are ready to write, whom are you going to thank? Perhaps you don't think there are many people to thank. At first it might feel that way, but once you start thinking about it you can create a long list.

To get started, write thank-you notes to family members. A thank-you letter would make a perfect present for any occasion. Once you've written family, consider who else has done something nice for you. Who takes you to school every day or places you need to go? Which friends deserve a big thank-you for being there for you? Who helps keep you healthy? Who teaches you things that help you learn and grow smarter? Who do you admire that deserves a thank-you?

Being a "Thank-You Kid" is a way of life. Once you get started writing thank-you notes, you'll see endless benefits. You'll also make other people feel good. Plus, by expressing your appreciation for others, the thank-yous will come back to you by the tons.

Chapter Two

Words of Thanks

I created the following lists to help make your job easy when writing a thank-you note, since we all need help now and then. In case you don't know what to say or find yourself wondering how to describe your feelings, check out the sections in this chapter for some amazing, wonderful, and incredible ideas that will help you put your feelings into words.

THANK-YOU WORDS FROM A TO Z

By adding some adjectives like the ones on the next pages, you'll instantly add some pizzazz to your letter writing. So next time you want to describe what the gift you received meant to you or even what you thought of it . . . check out this A–Z list for some astonishing, astounding, and awesome words to help you express a world of thanks!

A – admirable, adorable, amazing, appealing, astonishing, astounding, attentive, attractive, awesome

B – beautiful, bodacious, breathtaking, brilliant

C – captivating, caring, charming, colorful, compassionate, considerate, costly, crafty, cute

D – dazzling, dear, delicious, delightful, delightfully, divine

E – earth-shattering, elegant, enlightening, excellent, exceptional, exciting, exquisite, extraordinary

F – fabulous, fair, fantastic, fine, first-class, first-rate

G – gigantic, glorious, gorgeous, graceful, grand, gratifying, great

H – heartwarming, hearty, helpful, heroic, highly appreciated, hip, honorable

I – important, impressive, incredible, irreplaceable, irresistible

J – jamming, jolly

K – kind, kindly

L – likable, lovable, lovely

M – magical, magnificent, marveling, marvelous, matchless, miraculous

𝒩 – nice, nice-looking, notable, noteworthy

O – one of a kind, original, out of this world, out-standing, overboard

𝒫 – perfect, perfection, phenomenal, pleasurable, pretty, priceless

Q – quality, quaint

R – rare, remarkable, revered

S – selfless, smart, soul-warming, stunning, stupendous, superb, superior, superstar, surprising

T – terrific, thoughtful, tremendous

U – unique, unparalleled, unselfish, usable, useful

V – valuable, very

W – warm, well-beloved, well-loved, well-thought, wise, wonderful

X – x-tra (the word is really extra, but this is a fun version)

Y – your turn to think of something!

Z – zany, zippy

Creative Expressions

When it comes to writing a thank-you note, it's all about expressing your true feelings. Remember how you felt when you opened the gift? Or, ask yourself how much that person really means to you. Think about the time they spent choosing, wrapping, and sending you the gift. Your thank-you note is an opportunity to show how much it meant to you by expressing your thanks.

If for any reason you just don't know what to say, think of something special they taught you and express yourself from your heart. Tell Aunt Arlene how you enjoy spending time with her.

The following creative expressions are examples of things you could say when you write a thank-you note. Please keep in mind that it is important to say what you feel and, of course, really feel what you say!

Super Thank-You Sentences

Wow! I couldn't believe my eyes
when I opened your gift.

Your gift put a big smile on my face.

It was a special day when your gift arrived.

Your gift was exactly what I wanted!

You should have seen the expression
on my face when I saw your gift.

How can I ever thank you for the beautiful gift?

How can I ever thank you for being the perfect host?

I have a heart full of thanks for your
good deeds and wishes.

My thanks to you are endless.

I appreciate you more than words can ever say.

Your friendship is as good as gold.

A giant thank-you to such a special friend.

A great big thank-you from the bottom of my heart.

I wish I could be there in person to give you
the biggest thanks in the whole wide world.

You must be a mind reader, because you gave
me a gift I have always wanted.

Congratulations! You gave me a first-prize present.

Your gift defines the word amazing.

I'll never forget your generosity.

Your thoughtful deeds are the greatest gift of all!

A truckload of thanks for everything you have done.

I am overflowing with thanks for your thoughtfulness.

Your gift exceeded my imagination.

Your gift put a smile on my face, and your
wishes put a smile in my heart.

Whoa! I will really enjoy your totally awesome gift.

It would take me all day to thank you
for your really neat gift.

Your thoughtful deeds will go down in history!

SAY THANK YOU WITH A COMPLIMENT!

My warmest thanks to a real jewel.

How do I thank someone as precious as you?

Thank you to one of my most treasured friends.

No one can outshine your kindness or good deeds.

You are someone I really value spending time with.

You are one of my favorite people of all time.

You are one of the smartest people I know.

You always know the perfect thing to say and do.

*You have outdone yourself with your
incredible gift. Of course, you always do.*

Your outstanding taste is reflected in your fabulous gift.

*I will always treasure your gift and most of all
the beautiful thoughts that came with it.*

*A special person like you deserves the
biggest thank-you on earth.*

Leave it to you to find the coolest gift on the planet.

*Every time I look at your gift, I will think
of your unending kindness.*

*You are one in a million, and I'm
so lucky to call you my aunt.*

*My thanks to you for being someone
I can count on no matter what.*

Creative Closings

I always like to end my thank-you notes on a positive note, and there are many ways to do that. If you are writing a thank-you note to someone special, consider signing your note or letter with a creative expression.

The following closings are favorite examples of mine that I hope you'll enjoy using. Ending your thank-you note with a unique closing creates a special memory, and it will be a thank-you note they'll cherish forever!

Super Ways to Sign Off!

With a heart filled with thanks,

With hugs and smiles,

Forever friends,

Miles of smiles,

Best buds forever,

Just a call away,

Your pal,

Warm wishes,

Hope to see you soon,

Love and kisses,

Much love,

Forever yours,

With thanks always,

With hugs always,

Best friends for life,

Millions of thanks,

Forever thanks,

With extreme appreciation,

Sincerely,

A zillion thanks,

Your biggest fan,

Your good buddy,

Love you forever,

Too cool,

Your pen pal,

I love, love, love you,

You're the best,

Pen pals forever,

You're always on my mind,

Hugs and kisses,

With unending appreciation,

With unending thanks,

You're a star in my life,

See you soon,

Just a hop, skip, and jump away,

Sincerely yours,

Hugs and kisses coming at you,

Happiness and peace always,

Tons of thank-yous,

Smiles for life,

Good health and happiness all around,

A gigantic thank-you,

A sunshine thank-you,

A world of thanks,

A candy-coated thank-you,

WHAT'S IN A NAME?

Here are some fun ways to take the person's name you are thanking and make it part of your thank-you note. Each letter in his or her name should say something you feel describes that person. Here goes:

JANIE:
Just
About the
Nicest
Individual on
Earth.

LORIE:
Lovable
Original
Really
Incredible and
Exciting.

JUSTIN:
Just
Understanding
Super
Terrific
Irresistible &
Nice.

CARLA:
Caring
And
Really
Loving
Adult.

DAD:
Dedicated
And
Devoted.

MOM:
My
One and only
Marvelous Mom.

AUNT:
Always
Utterly
Nice and
Terrific.

UNCLE:
Unbelievable
Nice
Caring
Loving
Example.

TEACHER:
Terrific
Educator
Always
Caring about
Her
Excellent
Results.

OR PERHAPS YOU CAN MAKE A PLAY ON WORDS, USING THEIR NAMES AS WELL.

Great Scott!

You made your Mark!

You're a Genie out of a bottle,
because you made my wishes come true.

Leave it to Lois!

Mary, Mary, you are very . . .

Al, that's my pal!

You're a Jack-pot of a grandpa!

I believe in Steven.

Always ready is our Bettye!

If anyone can, Dan can.

You were Just-in time.

Chapter Three

Thank You for the Gift

Whenever someone takes the time to give you a gift, it's a gift in itself to send a thank-you note. Writing a thank-you note or letter is a creative way to express your feelings, and it also makes the person feel really appreciated for what they did.

No matter how you express your thanks, what matters is that the person who is being thanked should feel their thoughtfulness is acknowledged. Whenever you write a thank-you note, consider how you really felt when you received the gift. Your thank-you note will serve as a boomerang, returning good feelings and joy right back to the sender.

The following examples of thank-you notes will give you a jump start whenever you are writing one yourself. Your goal is to make someone feel good about his or her efforts, and all it takes is a little thought and creativity.

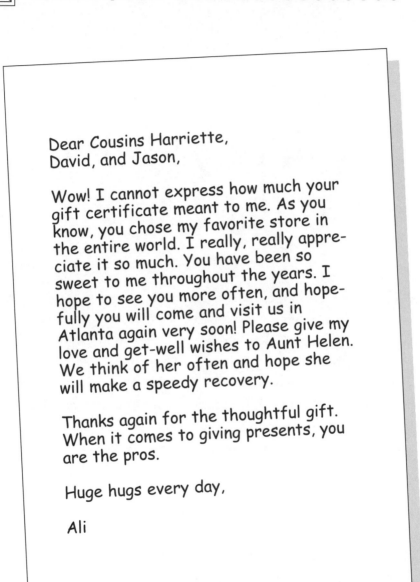

Dear Cousins Harriette,
David, and Jason,

Wow! I cannot express how much your gift certificate meant to me. As you know, you chose my favorite store in the entire world. I really, really appreciate it so much. You have been so sweet to me throughout the years. I hope to see you more often, and hopefully you will come and visit us in Atlanta again very soon! Please give my love and get-well wishes to Aunt Helen. We think of her often and hope she will make a speedy recovery.

Thanks again for the thoughtful gift. When it comes to giving presents, you are the pros.

Huge hugs every day,

Ali

Dear Rachel,

I would like to extend my gratitude for the beautiful crystal vase you sent me for my birthday. Words cannot express how much this gift and you mean to me. It will always remind me of you. You are one of the sweetest people I know, and I love being around you. I would also like to thank you for being a good friend. You have been a great buddy to me and we share something really special in common.

Your friend forever,

Jessica

Dear Lorie, Carla, and Janie,

When you arrived at our door with your spectacular gift, I was so surprised. The fact that you delivered it in person meant so much to me, and I really love the hand-made frame. It was so clever and thoughtful of you to put my photo-graph in it, and it's a work of art we will always appreciate. Your families mean the world to me and I think I'm a lucky girl to know you!

With a picture-perfect thank-you,

Ali

Dear Maya,

Thank you so much for the cookies and flowers. I really appreciate you thinking of me when I was ill. I am feeling better now and hope to see you soon.

Please tell your sister Amy that I said hi. You did very well at your soccer game! I was so impressed watching you play, and am glad to be back in the swing of things.

Thank you for your wishes,

Michelle

Dear Uncle Sam,

Thank you so much for the shares of stock you gave me on my birthday. I really appreciate them a lot. I promise to follow that stock every day!

I would also like to thank you for being a wonderful great-uncle and a great doctor, too. Whenever I am sick you always help us, even if it is 2:30 in the morning. You have always encouraged me to succeed in whatever my heart is set on doing. I love you so much and that will never ever change.

Your favorite and only niece,

Ali

Dear Samantha,

Where are all the words to describe
how much the silver engraved bracelet
you sent meant to me? Every time I
wear it I will think of you, and it is so
beautiful.

I would also like to thank you for being
a special friend. While you live in a different city, I feel like you're right
next door.

Again, thank you for a gift I will always
treasure.

Hope to see you soon,

Courtney

Dear Aunt Genie and Uncle Doug,

Words cannot express how much your check meant to me. It was so generous and really made my day. I used it to buy a phone, and as you know I am on the phone 24/7.

You two have done everything to make me happy and I really appreciate it so much. You are always there to support me in everything that I do, and you are a great aunt and uncle. I love you two so much. I always think of how sweet, kind, loving, and caring you are to my family and me! You are such a special aunt and uncle, and I'm one lucky kid to have you as mine.

Love always,

Your niece Ali

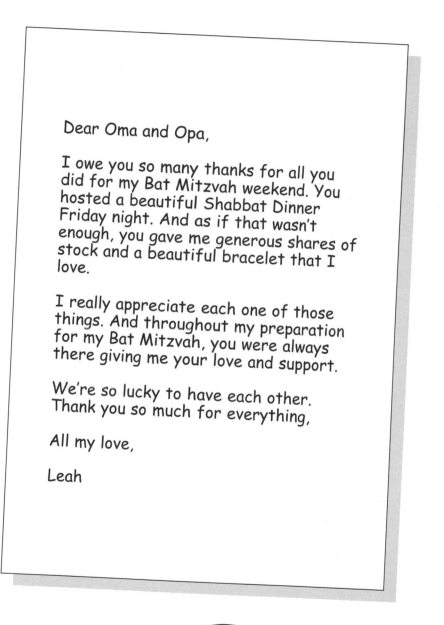

Dear Oma and Opa,

I owe you so many thanks for all you did for my Bat Mitzvah weekend. You hosted a beautiful Shabbat Dinner Friday night. And as if that wasn't enough, you gave me generous shares of stock and a beautiful bracelet that I love.

I really appreciate each one of those things. And throughout my preparation for my Bat Mitzvah, you were always there giving me your love and support.

We're so lucky to have each other. Thank you so much for everything,

All my love,

Leah

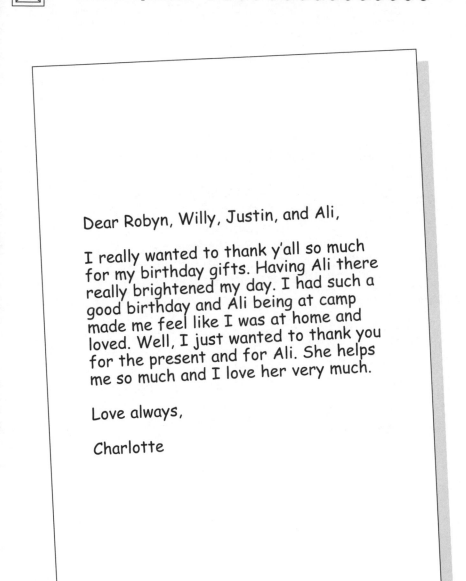

Dear Robyn, Willy, Justin, and Ali,

I really wanted to thank y'all so much for my birthday gifts. Having Ali there really brightened my day. I had such a good birthday and Ali being at camp made me feel like I was at home and loved. Well, I just wanted to thank you for the present and for Ali. She helps me so much and I love her very much.

Love always,

Charlotte

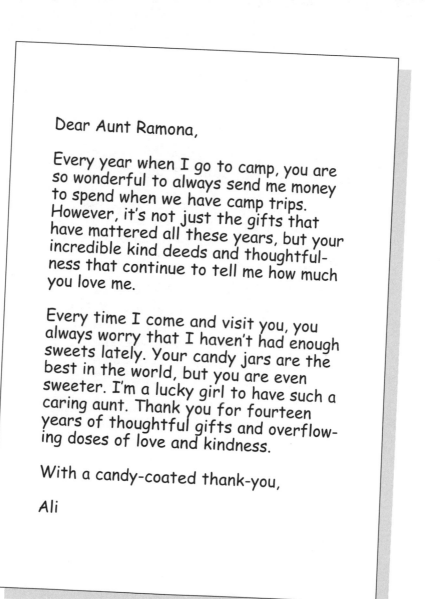

Dear Aunt Ramona,

Every year when I go to camp, you are so wonderful to always send me money to spend when we have camp trips. However, it's not just the gifts that have mattered all these years, but your incredible kind deeds and thoughtfulness that continue to tell me how much you love me.

Every time I come and visit you, you always worry that I haven't had enough sweets lately. Your candy jars are the best in the world, but you are even sweeter. I'm a lucky girl to have such a caring aunt. Thank you for fourteen years of thoughtful gifts and overflowing doses of love and kindness.

With a candy-coated thank-you,

Ali

Dear Robyn, Willy, Justin, and Ali,

Thank you so much for the graduation gift. I appreciated it so much. The money will come in handy at Arizona State University.

I really enjoyed your visit. I was so glad that you guys could make it to the wedding. You added so much to the experience. I hope you enjoyed the visit and I hope you will come down to Arizona. Thanks again for the graduation gift.

Love,

Casey

[Here's a thank-you note that my teacher Mrs. Tropauer saved in her special thank-you box. She let me borrow it back a year later for my book!]

Dear Eileen and Alan,

I appreciate the awesome Kate Spade bag! I love the bag and will cherish it forever. I'm so sorry that you could not come to my special event, but I hope, Eileen, that you feel so much better.

I hope to see you soon. You are the best teacher on earth!

With a million hugs,

Ali Spizman

Dear Arlene, Marshall, Austin, Elliott, Lala, Steve, Emily, Eleanor, and Aunt Ruth,

Your magnificent necklace took my breath away. When I opened the famous blue box I knew immediately that this was a gift I would always treasure. You have such wonderful taste and when I wear this necklace everyone will know it, too!

You all mean the world to me and I can't thank you enough for your generous gifts and best wishes for my happiness. You always think of me in such special ways, and once again you outdid yourselves. I love seeing you and am counting the days until we get together again.

You are a rainbow in my life and, even though we don't see each other often, you are always in my thoughts.

With Texas-sized hugs,

Ali

$$ Thank You for the Check $$

Sometimes, you are sent a gift that is a check or money. Instead of just saying "thank you for the check," there are many ways to creatively say thank you. Here are some ideas that will get you started and help you out just in case you don't know where to begin.

CHECK THESE SAYINGS OUT:

◎ How did you know that a check would be the perfect gift for a kid like me? I can't begin to thank you enough since I was saving up for a new baseball glove. Thanks to you and your generous gift, my greatest wish will soon come true.

◎ I was so grateful that you sent me a check for my graduation. It will be put in my college fund, and for that gift the entire family says thank you!

◎ Your thoughtful check was the perfect gift for a kid like me. I have always wanted a computer, and thanks to you I am well on my way towards reaching my goal.

◎ When I opened your envelope and gazed my eyes on that fabulous check, I couldn't believe what I saw. Your gift was so wonderful and I will always remember your generosity.

◎ When I opened your birthday card and saw the thoughtful check made out to my name, I almost fainted. Your gift will always be appreciated, and I promise to put it to a very good cause . . . me!

◎ The check you sent put me into orbit. That was so incredibly generous of you to think of me in such a big way. Your gift was out of sight!

◎ I'm saving up for a special camera, and your check will finally help me reach my goal. I promise to send you a picture of my family when I learn how to use it!

◎ Your check knocked me over with excitement. It was the perfect gift for a girl like me who loves to buy clothes. I promise to select an outfit that's very stylish and think of you every time I wear it!

Chapter Four

Thank You for the Hospitality

It is so nice when you receive an invitation to go to someone's home, out to dinner as their guest, or even to just get together. Over the years, many friends have been so generous and taken me to Braves games, to their farmhouses, to my favorite restaurants, or invited me to stay over when my parents were out of town.

It's such a treat when friends and family members invite you into their home or entertain you. These acts of kindness definitely deserve a thank-you note that lets them know how much they are appreciated.

I'll never forget when we took my friend Charlotte on a beach vacation with us to Hilton Head, South Carolina; she sent three thank-you notes and some amazing gifts to express her thanks. She wanted us to know what a great time she had, and her thank-you notes were really appreciated.

The following notes will help you get your point across when you want to say thank you for the hospitality.

Dear Aunt Lois and Uncle Jerry,

Thank you soooooooo much for thirteen great years of hospitality at your vacation house in Hilton Head! I've had <u>so</u> many wonderful summer memories there, thanks to you!

I also would like to express my gratitude for all you have done throughout the years. Words cannot even express how much I appreciate you both. I am very grateful to have such sweet, kind, loving, and caring people as you two in my life. If you hadn't already been related to me, I would have picked you out as family. You will always be in my heart. I love you so much!

A wave of thanks,

Ali

Dear Nina and family,

Thank you for the outstanding hospitality. You were there for my every need and I really appreciate it so much. You are so sweet. Nina is a lucky girl to have wonderful parents as nice as you.

Tulsa is a very nice city, and if you lived in Atlanta, I think that you would be very close friends with us. We all have a lot in common and maybe one day you will move here. For now, we'll just be long-distance friends forever.

Thank you for taking me out to lunch and driving us all around Tulsa, showing us every part of your beautiful city. From Holland Hall to Swann Lake, I had a blast seeing everything.

I can't wait to see Nina at camp, and thank you once again for being such sweet and kind friends and taking me in for the weekend as one of your own!

Hugs and Kisses,

Ali L. Spizman

Dear Vicki and Gilbert,

I would like to express my gratitude for all the times you have let me stay at your house. You both have treated me as if I am another daughter.

I also appreciated it when you acted like doctors to help make my hand feel so much better when I was sick at your house. Your touch worked like magic.

You two are sweet to my parents and me, and it really means a lot to all of us! You guys are friends that we will always adore!

With much love always,

Ali Spizman

Dear Ashley and Dean,

While attending your wedding, I thought I was with Cinderella and Prince Charming at the ball. It was beautiful and I am glad that I could share this special time with you. It meant the world to me to be included, and I loved every second of it.

I am so glad to know such a sweet, kind, loving, and caring couple.

Here's to your happiness,

Ali Spizman

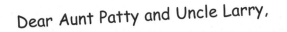
Dear Aunt Patty and Uncle Larry,

I really appreciated you hosting that magnificent dinner on Memorial Day. I am 100% sure that everyone enjoyed it, especially me. I got a chance to be with a lot of people who I usually don't see on a normal basis. Plus, dinner was really delicious. You are so sweet and kind to involve my family. We all think you both are a pretty amazing pair.

Throughout my life you have been so nice and concerned about me. Thanks for taking me everywhere, from the basketball games where Lisa cheerleaded to just out for ice cream late at night. I treasure all our times together.

With much gratitude,

Ali Spizman

Dear Erica,

It meant so much to me when you called to invite me to the concert. I was so sorry that I couldn't go, but I had very big Science and English tests the next day.

I'm so glad that we are friends. I also am glad that we live in the same neighborhood. I love riding bikes with you every chance we get. Thanks for all the great invitations.

Friends for life,

Ali

Dear Ashley,

Thank you so much for inviting me to your lake house. I really appreciated the offer and I had so much fun. I loved waterskiing and just riding on the boat and talking to you. I also loved sitting by the fire and toasting marshmallows. Since we went to the lake house, I feel that our friendship has gotten so much closer and I really cherish it. Also, please say thank you to your parents for having me. They are so sweet and you are a lucky girl to have such nice parents.

Friends for life,

Shoshana

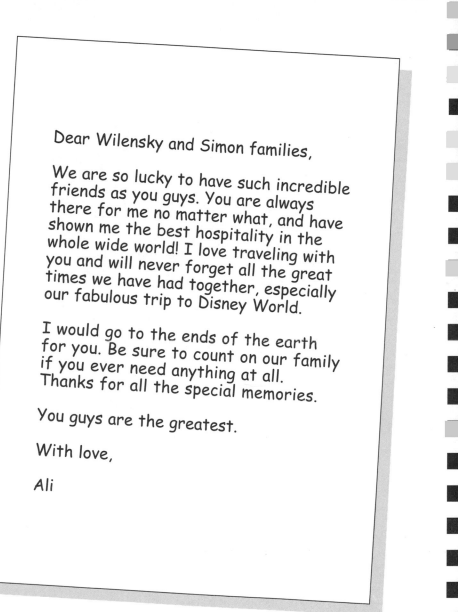

Dear Wilensky and Simon families,

We are so lucky to have such incredible friends as you guys. You are always there for me no matter what, and have shown me the best hospitality in the whole wide world! I love traveling with you and will never forget all the great times we have had together, especially our fabulous trip to Disney World.

I would go to the ends of the earth for you. Be sure to count on our family if you ever need anything at all. Thanks for all the special memories.

You guys are the greatest.

With love,

Ali

Dear Spizman Family,

Thank you so much for inviting my brothers, my friends, and me to the party. We all had so much fun! Meeting "Mr. Belding" was a dream come true. It is still what my friends and I talk about.

I really appreciate you taking the time to personally introduce all of us. It was so sweet, and I will never forget that moment. My family is so lucky to have such wonderful friends. Thanks again!

Love,

Gena

Chapter Five

Thank You, Family

Writing your family is very important, either to thank them for something that they did or to tell them that you love them. These thank-you notes and letters will become treasured messages for an entire lifetime.

I hope the letters presented in this chapter will inspire you to write meaningful letters that tell someone you love how they have made a difference in your life. It's the little things that often mean the most, so don't forget to thank someone you care about for those endless carpools, hundreds of meals, bedtime stories, the times you shared, and loads of other forgotten deeds.

Over the years, my family has saved letters that my brother and I wrote.

In fact, as you walk through our house, you'll find artwork from our childhood framed and even letters we wrote proudly displayed. You'll even see a few in this chapter. I hope the following ideas will help you get started writing gifts of thanks to those you care about. I promise that your thank-you letters will be the best gifts you could ever give your family!

Dear Mommy,

Wow, I have so much to thank you for. Overall, I would just like to thank you for being the best mom in the whole wide world. You have done everything you can to make me happy and I really appreciate it so much. I always have so much fun with you wherever we go, and you are so much fun to be with.

You have always been there standing by and ready to help me. You are also a great person to talk to. I can go to you about any problems I have, and I think that we have a mother-daughter relationship and friendship that will never end! I love you <u>so</u> much!

Your #1 daughter and biggest fan,

Ali

[Believe it or not, here's a letter my mom saved that I wrote when I was seven years old.]

Dear Mommy,

Thanks for having two children. Thanks for doing all those girl things with me. I always have a great time with you. Thanks for being so understanding when I do something wrong. I love you soooo much.

Your Favorite Girl,

Ali

Dear Daddy,

I would like to thank you for being the best dad in the whole wide world. I love going to baseball, football, and basketball games with you and especially when I drag you to the mall. I <u>always</u> have so much fun, even if we are just washing cars. You always look out for me and are there ready to help me in every way.

You are always willing to talk to me about whatever is on my mind and I also really value that. Our father-daughter friendship is so special to me and I cherish it far beyond words! I love you <u>so</u> much.

You are the best dad a girl could ever have!

Love always,

Ali

[And here's a letter my dad saved that I wrote when I was seven years old.]

Dear Daddy,

I love you so much. From the time that I opened my eyes and saw you, I knew that I would love you forever. I love it when we do daddy-daughter stuff together. I love it when we wash the cars together. You're the best dad a girl could have.

I love you,

Ali

Dear Justin,

I would just like to thank you for being a great brother! Through thick and thin, you have always been there for me no matter what.

I would also like to thank you for being my role model in a hundred different ways. I hope to always follow in your footsteps. You are such a great, sweet, kind, and loving person. You have taught me everything a big brother could teach a little sister, from learning to shoot a basketball to memorizing my multiplication tables. I hope you know how much I appreciate it!

Your biggest fan,

Your sister Ali

Dear Grandma and Honey,

How can I ever begin to thank you for everything that you have done for me? From taking me to the movies to taking me shopping and on outings, you two are the best. I love going over to your house every Friday night, and those lucky days in between where I get to say a little hello.

You two have been there for me whenever I needed you and even there just to talk to. I love spending time with you! I love you guys so much, and feel like the luckiest kid in the whole wide world.

Your #1 granddaughter,

Ali

Dear Papa Gus,

I love you so much. Thank you for coming to my school play, even though I knew it was hard for you because you aren't feeling well. I knew that you would love it. I love coming over to visit you, because seeing you with a smile on your face puts an even bigger smile on mine.

All my love,

Ali

[Even though my Grandma is gone, I still
love to remember her. I keep this letter in
a special place.]

Dear Nina,

I love you so much. Even though you
passed away in 1992, I still think that
you are here with us today. I miss you
so much and wish that I could see you
one last time.

You brought so much joy into my life
and I feel that I have so much of you
in me. You were a great grandma and
always thought of others.

I will never forget you.

With love always,

Ali

Dear Bettye,

I just wanted to tell you how thankful I am to have you in my life. I love you so much, and because of you I am who I am today! I love coming home to your presence and you always brighten up my day! You are like an angel. You are sweet, loving, caring, and always looking at the good side of everything!

You always help me when I need you. You are also one of the best role models in my life! I wish that everybody could grow up to have your perfect personality! Once again, I love you so much. I wrote this letter to tell you how I care about you, love you, and that you mean <u>so</u> much to me in my life. When I grow up, I want to have your personality.

I love you so much!

Love always,

Ali

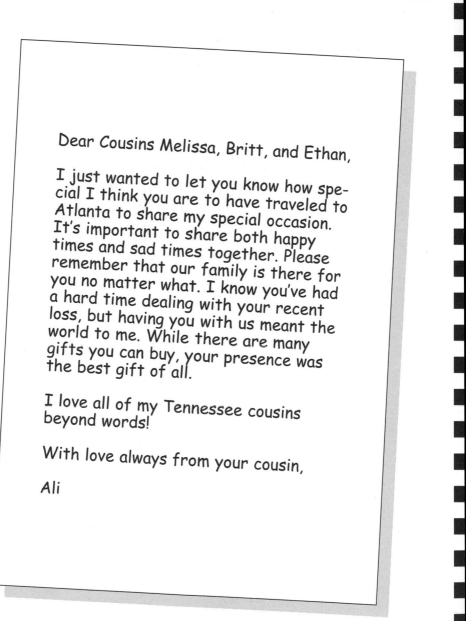

Dear Cousins Melissa, Britt, and Ethan,

I just wanted to let you know how special I think you are to have traveled to Atlanta to share my special occasion. It's important to share both happy times and sad times together. Please remember that our family is there for you no matter what. I know you've had a hard time dealing with your recent loss, but having you with us meant the world to me. While there are many gifts you can buy, your presence was the best gift of all.

I love all of my Tennessee cousins beyond words!

With love always from your cousin,

Ali

[Here's a letter my mom saved that my brother Justin wrote her while he was at college. He told her how much her lessons about saving money have meant to him. Even though I am only fourteen years old, I have learned that saving is important, too, and I liked Justin's letter a lot. It also made my mom feel really good. I also researched the concept of compound interest and learned that Albert Einstein said, "Compound interest is the single greatest force in the universe." To me that means every penny can add up—so don't waste money, because if you learn how to invest it, you can actually make it grow!]

Dear Mom,

I am writing you this letter to extend a thank-you for one of the most valuable lessons you taught me. As a young man, you told me again and again the importance of planning for my own future at a young age and truly understanding the idea of compound interest and saving my money. At first I shrugged off the idea and did not really pay attention to you. However, over the past year or so, I began thinking about this idea that you have repeated many times.

Thanks to you, I began investing the money I earned last summer in the stock market and truly began to understand how compound interest works. I learned that by planning my future at a young age, I can truly flourish and succeed as a young adult and hopefully one day become a financially independent person. I have learned the basic concept of conserving money and have become an individual who wants to earn money, rather than one who excessively spends it.

Thank you very much for teaching me this valuable lesson (excuse the pun). I will never forget it and will always save money and make smart decisions with my assets.

Love,

Justin

[Here's another letter I saved that my brother wrote to me for my Bat Mitzvah. It was printed in the morning's program and was a big surprise to me. Hundreds of people attending read it before I even saw it, and it became a gift I will always treasure.]

Dear Ali,

For the first six years of my life, I often heard the term, "Good things come in small packages." The cliché term was hard for a six-year-old boy to hear, especially one who wanted his parents to buy him ice-cream sundaes, the largest He-Man action figures, and the most enormous Transformer collection ever. I carried this notion until November 7, 1986, the day Ali was born. Looking back at that moment when I saw all 6 lbs. 7 oz. of my sister, I instantly understood the deeper meaning of this often-used cliché. I found that in my life, not only have good things come in small packages, but the best thing in my life, my sister, came in a small package.

My sister Ali is truly a gift to everyone with whom she has contact. She is the most loving, caring, kindhearted individual I have ever met. As ironic as it may seem, although she may not be able to hit a last-second shot like Michael Jordan, or strike a soccer ball with

the accuracy of Pelé, she has a way of walk-
ing into a room and immediately shining a magnificent ray of sunshine upon each individual
with whom she converses.

Though this day is the official transition to
adulthood, Ali has been an adult longer than I
think I have. She holds herself with an unbelievable level of maturity. While Ali carries the
notion that at age thirteen she knows everything, however funny as it may seem, what Ali
may not realize is that she has certain skills
that cannot be taught, ones many people may
never learn, no matter how old they are. Ali is a
special girl with a special way about her.

I would like to end with a personal reflection
to my sister. Congratulations, Ali, on your special day. If you look out over the congregation
while you are sitting on the bimah, you will see
hundreds of people whom you have impressed,
motivated, and astounded with your accomplishments. The first thirteen years of your life
have been a success, and if the rest of your
life continues on the same pathway, there are
no limitations to the things you can and will
achieve.

Love,

Justin

[Here's a letter that I hid in my mom's suitcase when I was nine years old and she went on a trip. She always surprises me with little notes, so I did the same for her!]

Dear Mom:

I hope that you have a fun time in Washington. I love you so much and hope that you have a great and safe trip. You are the best mommy a kid could have and I am so lucky to have you.

Thank you for loving me the way that you do.

With love and hugs waiting for you at home,

Ali

Dear May-May,

Every time I see you, you always put a huge smile on my face. You are so sweet and kind and I love you so much. You take such wonderful care of me and my family, and we have shared so many special times. Thank you for teaching me so many special things. You are an important part of our family and I treasure the time we spend together.

Hugs and kisses,

Ali

Here are some of my school friends for life!

Chapter Six

Thank You, Friend

One of the most important things in life is friendship. Friends can make lives so much sweeter. There are many occasions and times where you could say thank you to a friend. It doesn't take a lot to express your feelings so whenever you get a chance, just do it. It will make that person feel very good about themselves and feel appreciated. Saying thank you to someone will brighten their day and yours, too!

The following thank-you notes are ones that I have written for my friends. Friends are one of life's greatest gifts, and I hope my friends know how much they mean to me! Now it's your turn to thank a friend. Read these letters to get you started.

Dear Meredith,

You are such a great friend. You have always been there to support me in every way. From the farm (that yucky "red" house) to the beach, we've been through it all!

Since I don't have a sister, you earned that name. We have a certain relationship that will never change, no matter what, even if we are 1,000 miles apart. I will still always take the time to call you and say hello. You always brighten up my day, and I feel so lucky to have a friend like you. I love you so much, not just as a sis, but as a best friend.

Sincerely,

Ali

Dear Alli,

Friends like you are one in a million, and I can't begin to thank you enough for being there for me and adding so much happiness to my life. That's what best friends are for! We have known each other for eleven years and that special friendship we have will never end.

Whatever would I do without your brilliant opinion and insightful wisdom? Thank you, Alexander Graham Bell, for inventing the telephone, and thank you, Alli, for the millions of times we shared long talks on it.

We have been through a lot together as best friends.

Best friends forever and ever,

Ali

Dear Brittany,

You have been so sweet to me, so much more than I have asked for! Here is a poem that I wrote for you:

I'm always glad that I am home,
When you call me on the telephone.
So thank you for your thoughtful ways,
For brightening up all my days.
Thank you for the love you show,
For all the caring you bestow.
Your friendship means so much to me,
It will never end when we are 103!

Brittany, I am so glad to have a friend like you! You always care about others before yourself, and you're always there to put a smile on someone's face. I loved the time when we were snowed in at my house and we made up dances, ate, and just sat around and talked. You are a friend that I will always treasure!

Best friends forever,

Ali

To all my guy friends,

I'm a very lucky girl to have such a great group of friends. You are the best guy friends that anyone could ever have. I hope you all know who you are, but just in case, be sure to ask me! I love talking to you because all of you are the best listeners on earth. You are also really funny and know the right times to make me laugh! My friendship with each of you is so important to me, and I hope we all stay friends for years to come.

Friends forever,

Ali

Dear Charlotte,

I will always remember all the special times we have spent together. We've had fantastic memories with each other, from being at camp to just sitting around at home. I love being with you! You are a perfectly wonderful friend and I treasure you.

Thank you for always being there for me. You make me laugh when I am sad, you comfort me when I am worried, and you are a great person to talk to when I need to talk. You are someone that I can always count on. I love you so much!

Best friends till the end of time,

Ali

Dear Hilary and Stephanie,

Thanks for being such great friends.
Here's a poem just for you:

Roses are red,
Violets are blue,
Nothing's better
Than friends like you!

I hope that you like the poem, because
you are both true-blue friends to me!

Friends Always,

Ali

Dear Ally,

We have been great friends since pre-school and I've loved every minute of our friendship. From modeling to dance lessons, we've done it all.

I am so glad that I have you as a best friend, because you are always there for me. When I need to talk or laugh, you are standing by. I know that our friendship is something special and will never change.

Longtime best buds,

Ali

Dear Rachel,

One of the things I appreciate about you most is that you always extend a welcoming heart to anyone who needs a friend! You are one of my best friends in the whole wide world and we share a special bond.

Through thick and thin, we have always been the best of friends. Words cannot describe how much our friendship means to me and how wonderful it is to have a friend like you. We are like two peas in a pod.

With big hugs for you,

Ali

Chapter Seven

Community Thank-Yous

There are so many people around our community who deserve a big thank-you. From teachers to doctors to other people who help you daily, there are many individuals who make your world a better place. Often these people who do so much for us go about their job without being thanked.

This chapter is very important, because if each one of us sent even one thank-you to someone who deserved it, the world would be a nicer place. Consider for a moment someone you could thank and write that person a note of your appreciation.

The following thank-you notes are to people whom I appreciate and who help me all the time. From my dentist who fixes my broken braces to my teachers who help me learn new things, I am very grateful to all of them. I hope these notes will encourage you to write to someone special in your life, too.

Dear Dr. Salama,

Thank you so much for always caring about my teeth. You are one of the best dentists in the whole wide world and you always put a huge smile on my face! I appreciate your nice compliments when I see you, and actually enjoy going to the dentist. I also love seeing Dr. Goldstein and Dr. Garber, plus everyone at your office is so nice to me.

You keep on fixing my braces until they are perfect. You're a really awesome dentist and I'm proud you are mine! Thanks once again for making my visits to the dentist really fun, fearless, and fortunately pain-free.

All smiles!

Ali

Dear Dr. Fuller,

I feel like a really lucky kid to have you as my doctor. I really appreciate how sweet and kind you are, especially when I come in with a sore throat or strep throat. Even when I feel rotten, you have a special talent for putting a smile on my face.

As much as I hate getting a shot, your nurses are quick with their stick and make it easy. Being a doctor is probably a really hard job, but you always find a way to make it enjoyable.

Thanks again for caring,

Ali Spizman

Dear Postman Dover,

Thank you so much for delivering our mail every day. It must be a really hard job to deliver mail to hundreds of mailboxes, checking all those addresses and getting it right. (You're perfect at that.) You always handle the mail with such care. When I go to the mailbox as soon as I see your mail truck, you always have a smile on your face. You are the best postman I know, and the Spizman family really appreciates everything you do for us daily.

Thanks for the perfect delivery,

Ali Spizman

Dear Longstreet Press,

I would like to extend my gratitude with a million thanks for publishing my book. I have always had a dream of writing a book, and because of you it has come true! I would also like to thank you for listening to my ideas. I know I'm only fourteen years old, but I promise I'll do my best.

I think you are an awesome publisher to believe in a kid. It shows you really understand my generation. I plan on making you proud and happy you are publishing my book. You have been so sweet and kind, and I can't thank you enough.

A heart filled with thanks,

Ali Spizman

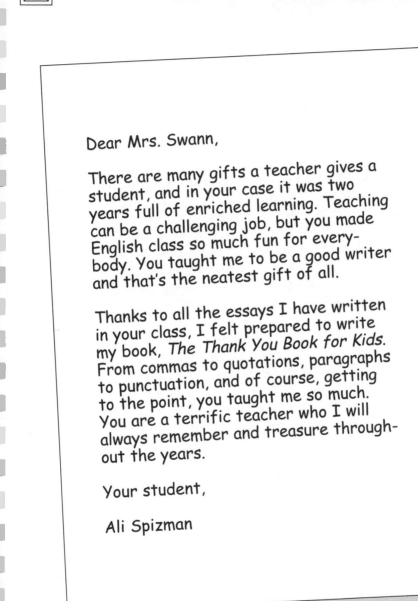

Dear Mrs. Swann,

There are many gifts a teacher gives a student, and in your case it was two years full of enriched learning. Teaching can be a challenging job, but you made English class so much fun for everybody. You taught me to be a good writer and that's the neatest gift of all.

Thanks to all the essays I have written in your class, I felt prepared to write my book, *The Thank You Book for Kids*. From commas to quotations, paragraphs to punctuation, and of course, getting to the point, you taught me so much. You are a terrific teacher who I will always remember and treasure throughout the years.

Your student,

Ali Spizman

Dear Mrs. Chesser,

I just wanted to write you a thank-you note to let you know what I appreciate about you as my 8th grade English teacher. You have a remarkable passion for what you teach. Your enthusiasm for William Golding, Chaim Potok, Voltaire, Rousseau, and many others is amazing. You even made grammar seem more interesting. This takes a special talent and you've got it. Shakespeare would have been proud of a teacher like you! I know I sure am!

With a grammatically correct thank-you,

Ali Spizman

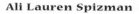

Dear Barby:

For the past few years you have answered my questions and assisted me in learning everything under the sun. From math to science and reading, you are just like Merlin the Magician, making all the answers appear. I feel very grateful to you for all the assistance you have given me, and my excellent grades in school reflect your hard work and what you've taught me.

Thanks also for all the treats and sweets that you've rewarded me with over the years. You sure know how to make a student smile.

Thanks for being a great teacher,

Ali

Dear Eileen,

You are a wonderful writing teacher and I am so lucky to be one of your students. You have opened up a true love of writing for me and I am very grateful. You are also such an amazing and dedicated teacher, and I appreciate everything you have taught me over the years.

Because I believe in saying thank you, I am now writing a book and hope you will help me accomplish my goal. I was wondering if you have saved any thank-you letters from your students? I was also wondering why saying thank you is so important to you, since you are such an appreciative and giving person.

Thank you so much for your time and attention, and I can't wait to hear back from you.

A very special thanks to a special person,

Ali Spizman

[Below is my teacher Eileen's response.]

Dear Ali,

From my earliest memories, reading became my world. Each new book excited me, and from that passion my life as a teacher was born. I immersed myself in the lives of imaginary characters and the pleasures of language that brought them to life. I taught the children and they, in turn, challenged me to continue to learn. Class was not a chore but a joy.

Yet teaching is double-edged—usually, a delight, occasionally, a frustration. One student might miss the poetic beauty of a Dickinson line, or a crisis in *Romeo and Juliet*, or the flow of language in *To Kill a Mockingbird*. Maybe a dangling participle dangled, despite my careful attempt to explain it . . . and it remained a mystery. Sometimes I just had a headache. My mentor, a seasoned English teacher, confided to me that on bad days she would read thank-you notes from grateful students who understood her own love for reading.

That evening, I found a small wooden box in the attic and began to fill it with thank-you notes for my own "bad" days.

Years passed as touching notes accumulated in my box. When struck with all the frustrations and moments of sadness that occur in every life at times, I revisit those wonderful words of my students. Their words remind me of the usefulness of my work, the contagious effect of my own enthusiasm for reading and writing, and my spirit is renewed.

Recently I recalled the heartening words of the famous French writer, Albert Camus: "In the depth of winter, I finally learned that within me there lay an invincible summer." He understood that, even in trying times, sadness can never extinguish the joy within us. And the words of my students touch that chord of joy within me, reminding me of the one gift I had always hoped to give them . . . a love for the beauty of literature—its magic, its language, its "invincible summer."

Love,

Mrs. Tropauer (E.T.)

Chapter Eight

Writing Thank-You Letters to Famous People

I have always enjoyed writing letters to famous people. I love to collect their autographs, and sometimes they will send you a signed picture of themselves, too. Although I'm sure most of them get tons of fan mail, you never know when you just might make their day. So when I began writing this book, it was the perfect excuse for me to write a whole bunch of famous people I admire.

From Rosa Parks to Michael Eisner to dozens of other well-known individuals, my thank-yous were over-flowing and headed in many different directions. Each and every time I opened our mailbox, I searched through the mail to see if there were any replies for me. Once in a while, a letter with a famous address like The Walt Disney Company or The White House arrived at my door. What amazed me most was that the busiest people in the world still had time to write a kid in Atlanta, Georgia. Even the famous astronaut Eugene Cernan, who has set foot on the moon, wrote me back! What didn't surprise me, however, was the fact that these famous people also shared my belief that thank-yous are very important.

While not every celebrity had time to write me back a letter, some very famous people's offices called to say they were sorry they didn't have time to respond. I thought that was really nice. I also received some responses by fax, while others came through e-mail and the U.S. mail. I felt that it was extraordinarily kind of those individuals who took time from their busy days to share their feelings about saying thanks with us kids.

In case you would like to write someone famous, keep in mind that they are super busy. While some might have time to write you back, be sure to respect their privacy and be understanding in case they don't have time to reply. Here are some tips on writing famous people in case you want to try it yourself.

How to Find Famous People's Addresses

There are many ways to find the addresses of famous people. Here are some ways that worked for me:

VISIT YOUR LOCAL LIBRARY: That was my first stop. I asked the librarian how to reach famous people, and there are some very good books that include famous people's addresses. Famous people move just like the rest of us, so be sure to put your return address, just in case.

VISIT YOUR LOCAL BOOKSTORE: Next, I went to my local bookstore and asked the salesperson at the cash register if he knew of any books that would help me write to famous people. Here is one resource I located:

The Address Book: How to Reach Anyone Who Is Anyone by Michael Levine. This book gives you access to over 4,000 celebrities, corporate execs, and other VIPs.

SEARCH THE INTERNET: The Internet is my favorite place to search for names and addresses of famous people. I logged onto the popular site Ask Jeeves (www.ask.com) and that's where I found a very big list of celebrity and famous people's addresses. Just ask Jeeves where you can find celebrity addresses, and he'll help you out in a flash. You can also search for names through search engines.

You can also check out Ken Leebow's book series titled *300 Incredible Things to Do on the Internet,* which includes a book for students, parents, and teachers that he coauthored with my mom, Robyn Spizman. It's called *300 Incredible Things to Learn on the Internet.* You can find a list of his books at www.300Incredible.com. They can help you find everything on the Web from A to Z!

WRITE THEIR ORGANIZATION OR AGENT: Sometimes you have to write to the person who represents a famous celebrity. In the case of athletes, you might need to write their team. Sometimes a famous person has an agent who has a fan club department and other people answer all of their mail. Many celebrities have a staff that sends you back a form letter and an autographed picture. I think it's still fun to write.

The following letters represent some of the many I've written and received over the past few years.

Dear Michael Eisner:

My name is Ali Spizman and I know you receive a ton of letters, but I hope you'll see the importance of this letter and write me back soon. When my parents took me to Disney World, I thanked them at least a hundred times. Because I believe in saying thank you, I am writing a book and hope you will help me accomplish my goal. My book, which is just for kids, is all about 'saying thank you' and will come out in the spring of 2001.

Would you please consider sending me a letter that tells kids why saying thank you is so important? Any words of encouragement that you can share with me will really be meaningful. I hope you will write me back. Remember that kids all over the world will be reading it and you just might help make the world a more thoughtful place!

Being an author is not an easy job, especially when you are only thirteen. I promise to do a great job, inspire kids to express their thanks, and will send you a copy.

With many thanks,

Ali Spizman

13 years old

 The (WALT DISNEY Company

Dear Ali:

Like most kids, I used to groan over having to write a thank-you note. I mean, it was always great to get a present, but then it seemed to kill all the fun when my parents made me sit down to neatly write out, "Dear Uncle Joe, thank you so much for your generous and thoughtful gift" and then have to even more neatly address the envelope.

Then, one day, I realized that I was thinking about this thank-you business all wrong. It suddenly occurred to me that a thank you is really a chance to give a gift back to someone who had given me a gift. And, the more meaningful or personal the thank-you, the better a gift it was. So, my thank-yous started reading more like, "Dear Uncle Joe, thank you so much for buying me the souvenir baseball at the Yankee game. It will always remind me of our special day together, especially since the Yankees won!" I actually started to look forward to writing these thank-you "gifts" because they were a chance to express what I really felt about the present and about the person who gave it.

I've tried not to forget this lesson. If someone gives me a gift, or if a co-worker does an especially good job, I always try to write a personal thank-you note. As with most things in life, when we put in a little extra effort it tends to be rewarding for everyone.

Ali, good luck on your book . . . and thank you for inviting me to participate!

Sincerely,

Michael D. Eisner

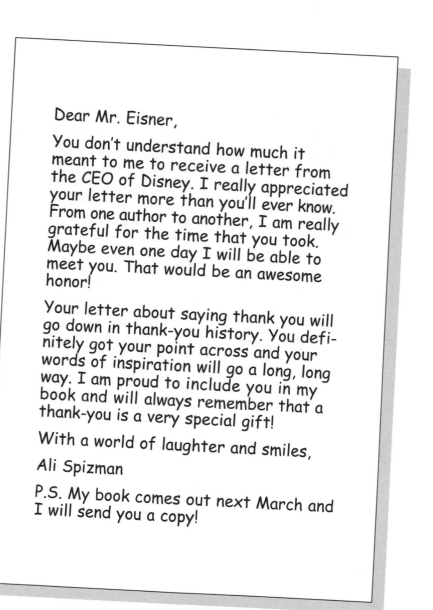

Dear Mr. Eisner,

You don't understand how much it meant to me to receive a letter from the CEO of Disney. I really appreciated your letter more than you'll ever know. From one author to another, I am really grateful for the time that you took. Maybe even one day I will be able to meet you. That would be an awesome honor!

Your letter about saying thank you will go down in thank-you history. You definitely got your point across and your words of inspiration will go a long, long way. I am proud to include you in my book and will always remember that a thank-you is a very special gift!

With a world of laughter and smiles,

Ali Spizman

P.S. My book comes out next March and I will send you a copy!

Dear Mr. Haskins:

Hi! It's Ali Spizman in Atlanta and I think you can really help me out! I am a big fan of yours and love watching you play Mr. Belding on *Saved by the Bell.* I am writing a book called *The Thank You Book for Kids.* My book will be for kids and I hope you will write me a letter to be included that will inspire kids.

Here's how you can help me. My book will encourage kids to say thank you. I hope you will send me a letter that tells kids why saying thank you is so important. Any words of encouragement that you share with kids will really be meaningful. I hope you will help me out and write me back. I promise to send you a copy.

I am so proud of you and hope you will write me back soon.

With a big thank-you,

Ali Spizman

13 years old

Why it's important to say thank you!

I have many thoughts on this subject, but the simplest is that it is the right thing to do.

Not everyone does things to get a thank-you but, when said, it is most appreciated. It validates that their efforts affected you in a way that meant something to you, more than just an everyday occurrence.

I was taught by my parents a long time ago to say "yes sir and no sir, yes ma'am and no ma'am." To me, these are basic tools to being polite.

Saying thank you goes beyond that. It is a little more effort to recognize that someone made a difference, on whatever level in your life, and it lets them share in that.

I remember, when I first got to Los Angeles, being in a musical as an understudy. For those of you who don't know what that is, you get to perform only if the person playing the role you are understudying doesn't go on for some reason. That rarely happens.

Another person in the show told me to send David Galligan a note at Drama-logue, a local industry newspaper, about my being in this musical and he might mention me in his column. I had just gotten to Hollywood and was looking for help wherever I could get it. David added me to his column the next week.

I called to say thank you and was amazed to hear that David was shocked to get the call. "No one ever calls to say thank you!" he said. We became friends and 8 years later I starred in a musical he was directing called *Angry Housewives* that lead to my being cast in *Good Morning, Miss Bliss,* which later evolved to become *Saved by the Bell.*

Now, I'm not saying that a thank-you will lead to your own television series, but it might lead to long-lasting friend-ships or, at the very least, to letting someone know that they made a difference in your life for a moment.

It takes so little effort and will be so warmly received. Try it! You'll like it!

Dennis Haskins

Chris Haston

Dear Dennis Haskins,

It meant so much to me to receive a letter from you to include in my book. I feel that when kids read your letter all over the world and hear that saying thank you could mean that much to someone, it will encourage them to say thank you themselves.

I really appreciate how sweet you have been to my family and me and it is so awesome to know you! You know that *Saved by the Bell* will always be one of my favorite shows, and as the one and only Mr. Belding . . . you will always be my favorite TV actor.

A million thanks,

Ali Spizman

Dear Mr. Ertegun:

I was so inspired to learn all about you. I am thirteen years old and currently writing a thank-you book for kids that will be published by Longstreet Press in 2001. My mom told me all the famous musicians you discovered and I was so amazed. You should be very proud of yourself.

I am writing because I am interested in knowing if you would be kind enough to write me a letter that I can include in my book about any of the famous musicians you know who always said thank you or were very thoughtful. Your letter or little story would impress kids and let them know that saying thank you is cool. My book is for little kids up to teenagers and will give examples of thank-you letters, notes, and other ways to say thank you. I hope it will make the world a nicer place.

Your letter would also be a credit to a good person you know and inspire others. I hope you will make time to write me back. I hope to hear from you.

Sincerely,

Ali Spizman

13-year-old author who LOVES music

Dear Ms. Spizman:

In spite of what you hear about famous singers and musicians' egos, all the musicians I have known possess a great virtue . . . humility.

The many letters and notes I have received of thanks from such great artists as Ray Charles, Otis Redding, Aretha Franklin, Mick Jagger, Bette Midler, Robert Plant, Phil Collins and Eric Clapton, have also been reciprocated by the thanks I have given them for their incredible contributions to me, my company Atlantic Records, and to the music world in general.

I thank all of my artists because without them, Atlantic Records would have never persevered.

Sincerely,

Ahmet M. Ertegun
Founder and Co-Chairman
Atlantic Records

Dear R. L. Stine:

My name is Ali Spizman and I am a really big fan and want to thank you for writing such great books. I tell all my friends to read your books. You are a really wonderful writer.

Like you, I will soon be an author and hope you'll help me accomplish my goal. Here's how you can help me. My book will encourage kids to say thank you. I hope you will send me a short letter that tells kids why saying thank you is so important. Any words of encouragement will really be helpful. Do you remember who taught you to say thank you? Are you thankful for all the kids who read your books? I hope you will help me out and write me back. Being an author is not an easy job, especially when you are only thirteen. I promise to do a great job, inspire a bunch of thank-yous, and will send you a copy.

With a great big GOOSEBUMP thank-you,

Ali Spizman

13 years old

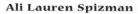

R.L. Stine

Kids write all the time to thank me for writing my books. I love reading their letters—but sometimes they're a little strange.

For example, a girl wrote this letter to me recently:

Dear R.L. Stine,

Thank you for writing such great books. I'm trying to collect all of your books. But I'm having trouble keeping up. Do you think you could stop writing for a while?

I had a good laugh at that one. She was thanking me— and asking me to stop at the same time!

ALI LAUREN SPIZMAN
"THE THANK-YOU KID"
May 20, 2000
TO: THE PRESIDENT OF HARVARD UNIVERSITY

Dear President Rudenstine:

Even though I am only thirteen years old, I am writing to you with a special request.

I will soon be an author and hope you will help me accomplish my goal. My book, which is just for kids, is all about saying "thank you" and will come out in the spring of 2001. Longstreet Press will be publishing it, and they are excited! It will be jam-packed with creative thank-you letters to inspire other kids to write. I have also written famous people and asked them the importance of saying thank you.

Here's how you can help me. I hope you will send me a short letter that tells kids why saying thank you is so important *even when they go off to college and gradu-ate.* Any words of encouragement that you can share with kids will really be meaningful. I hope you will help me out and write me back. Remember that kids will be reading it and you just might help make the world a more thoughtful place!

With many thanks,

Ali Spizman

13 years old

HARVARD UNIVERSITY

Dear Ali Lauren Spizman:

I am honored that you have asked me to talk about the very good topic you have raised: the importance of saying "thank you."

I say "thank you" all the time, and I couldn't be happier to do it. I thank foreign dignitaries for visiting Harvard. I thank my staff for the work they do to keep me on time and on schedule. I thank the students who work hard to represent the university well in their academic and sports pursuits. I thank my family for being supportive in my job as president. I thank people for their letters to me offering praise—and even when they offer criticisms! I thank people who send me gifts and good wishes. I thank the wonderful custodian in my office who goes out of his way to be sure that I have candy and cookies readily available when I go to the kitchen to get my coffee.

In short, thanking people not only expresses our gratitude, but it also fills us with a small sense of joy when we take the time to appreciate those around us. Just as when we step away from our busy lives to gaze at a painting in a museum or marvel at a sunset, we should likewise slow down to express our admiration and gratefulness for all the little things—and the big things—that people do every day to make our lives better.

And now, thank you, Ali for writing me! I send you—a very young author indeed—my warmest wishes for success with your book and with all your other pursuits in the years to come.

Sincerely,

Neil L. Rudenstine
President

Dear Wally Amos,

Hello. My name is Ali Spizman and I know you receive a ton of letters, but I hope you'll see the importance of this letter and please write me back soon. Since I was a baby I have always loved your Famous Amos Chocolate Chip Cookies!!!!! I could eat a whole box at a time. My favorite flavor is chocolate chip.

Because I believe in saying thank you, I am writing a book and hope you will help me accomplish my goal. My book, which is just for kids, is all about saying "thank you" and will come out in the spring of 2001. I hope you will write me back.

I would like to know why you think telling kids to say thank you is so important. Any words of encouragement that you can share with me will really be meaningful. Remember that kids all over the world will be reading it and you just might help make the world a more thoughtful place!

A chocolate-chip thank-you,

Ali Spizman

13 years old

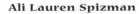

Dear Ali,

Congratulations on your book contract. You are very impressive and your subject matter is one of the most important you could have chosen.

A civilized society is based on manners, and "thank you" is the cornerstone of good manners. When you say thanks to someone it tells them that you appreciate and value them. It says you realize they took their precious time to honor a request or do some special deed just for you. Saying thank you acknowledges other people in your life. It also encourages people to do more for you.

There are also personal rewards from saying thank you. You feel better about yourself knowing you have given another human being something that money cannot buy. You have made someone feel special and appreciated. When I see people approaching me, I always like to imagine they have the initials MMFS, "Make Me Feel Special," on their forehead. So, when you say thank you, you make people feel special. "Thank you" are two of the most important words in the English language.

Thank you, Ali, for asking me to be a part of your book. I know it will help a lot of people and make them feel special.

Aloha from your chocolate-chip-cookie friend,

Wally Amos

Dear First Lady Hillary Clinton:

My name is Ali Spizman and I believe you are a "thank you" person. I was very inspired by how you have thanked people in your career and hope you'll consider writing me back. I will soon be a published author and hope you will help me accomplish my goal. My book, which is just for kids, is all about saying 'thank you' and will come out in the spring of 2001.

Would you please consider sending me a short letter that tells kids why saying thank you is so important? Any words of encouragement that you can share with kids will really be meaningful. I hope you will write me back. Remember that kids all over the world will be reading it and you just might help make the world a more thoughtful place!

With many thanks,

Ali Spizman

13 years old

THE WHITE HOUSE

WASHINGTON

Dear Ali,

Thank you for your thoughtful letter. I enjoy hearing from young people and reading about the things that interest and concern you.

I appreciate your sharing with me your thoughts about an issue that is important to you and to many other young people. Your comments are important to me.

Please stay interested in issues affecting our communities and our country, and continue to make your opinions known. Remember that you can make a difference.

Thank you for taking the time to write to me.

Sincerely yours,

Hillary Rodham Clinton

Hillary Rodham Clinton

Dear Rosa Parks:

I want to thank you for being such a remarkable inspiration to people of all ages around the world. Last year I read a book about your life during Black History Month and wrote a paper all about your life. Your refusal to give up your seat on the Montgomery bus was a great act of courage. You taught everyone not just to stand up for what you believe in, but to fight for it until you make a difference.

You have touched me deeply with your act of determination and bravery. It meant so much to see how one woman was so brave. You taught me that if you try to do the right thing, then others will follow. You are a true hero and a role model to all of us.

In your book you said, "Love, not fear, must be our guide." Those powerful words led me to believe that solving problems takes an open hand, not a closed fist. While no one probably thanked you that day on the bus, I wish to thank you from the bottom of my heart. Thank you for making a difference and showing us that one person can be heard.

With a world of belated thank-yous,

Ali Spizman

13 years old

I think Rosa Parks is really an amazing lady and I wrote a report about her for school last year. I hope she reads my book one day and knows that people all over the world think she is a really special and courageous woman. I'm proud of you, Rosa, and you deserve a world of thanks!

Dear J. K. Rowling,

Hello. My name is Ali Spizman and I know you receive tons of letters, but I hope you'll see the importance of this letter and I would love to receive a letter from you soon!

I have read your books and I have loved every minute of reading them. I just started reading your new one, *Harry Potter and the Goblet of Fire*. I can't wait to keep on reading it.

Because I believe in saying thank you, I am writing a book called *The Thank You Book for Kids*. It is going to be published by Longstreet Press in the spring of 2001. My book, which is just for kids, will be jam-packed with every kind of way to say thank you, and creative thank-you letters to inspire other kids to write more thanks. I would like to know why telling kids to say thank you is so important in your own opinion. And any words of encouragement that you can share with me will be meaningful. Remember that kids all over the world will be reading it and you just might help make the world a more thoughtful place!

I am excited to write my first book, especially at the age of thirteen. I promise to do a great job, inspire kids to express their thanks, and will send you a copy!

With many thanks,

Ali Spizman

13 years old

[J. K. Rowling wasn't able to write me back, but her publisher Scholastic wrote me a really nice letter and explained that the great popularity of Harry Potter and his author have resulted in extraordinary demands on Ms. Rowling's time. They wished me lots of luck with my book! I thought that was very kind of such a busy publisher.]

Dear Mark Victor Hansen:

My name is Ali Spizman and I am a really big fan and want to thank you for writing such great books. I tell all my friends to read your *Chicken Soup for the Soul* books. You are a really wonderful writer.

Here's how you can help me. I am writing a book that will encourage kids to say thank you. I hope you will send me a short letter that tells kids why saying thank you is so important. Any words of encouragement that you can share with kids will really be meaningful. Do you remember who taught you to say thank you? Or, have you ever received a thank-you for writing your stories that inspired you? I hope you will help me out and write me back.

Keep up the great work and I hope you will write me back soon.

With a great big Chicken Soup thank-you,

Ali Spizman

13 years old

[I was very excited to hear back from Mr. Hansen, who actually endorsed my book and shared this thought:

"*The more you are thankful for, the more you get to be thankful for.*"

I think that makes a lot of sense, and I'm thankful for the generous helping of *Chicken Soup for the Soul* books that Mark Victor Hansen has written. I especially love *Chicken Soup for the Teenager's Soul!*]

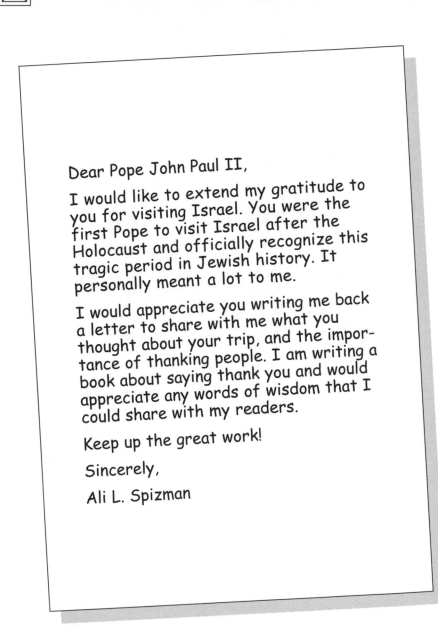

Dear Pope John Paul II,

I would like to extend my gratitude to you for visiting Israel. You were the first Pope to visit Israel after the Holocaust and officially recognize this tragic period in Jewish history. It personally meant a lot to me.

I would appreciate you writing me back a letter to share with me what you thought about your trip, and the importance of thanking people. I am writing a book about saying thank you and would appreciate any words of wisdom that I could share with my readers.

Keep up the great work!

Sincerely,

Ali L. Spizman

[Few people on earth have visited the moon, so I decided to write astronaut Eugene Cernan, who was the last man on the moon, and ask him for any wisdom or advice he has for kids.]

Ali Spizman

The Thank-You Kid

April 15, 1999

Dear Captain Cernan:

My name is Ali Spizman and I am twelve years old. I have learned all about you and really admire you! You made us all very proud, and I think it is awesome that you walked on the moon. All of us say thank you!

I probably won't make it to the moon, but I do hope to accomplish something right here on earth. I am writing a book just like you did and would like to include a letter from you.

(continued on next page)

— 2 —

I have learned so many things from the people in my life that I love, and I'm hoping to hear what you've learned from people you love, too. I know you're really busy, but I promise you'll be proud you took the time to share a lesson you learned from someone you love who made a difference in your life.

Thank you for your time, and I hope to hear from you soon! It means the world to me, and I think you will inspire others to make a difference in the life of some-one they love.

Sincerely,

Ali Spizman

Dear Ali:

Thank you for your very kind letter and for the nice things you said about me. After meeting your mother, I understand where you get your enthusiasm. I want to particularly commend you for the commitment you have made in carrying out your book writing project. It is an honor for me to be included.

Although I'm quite sure you will become a very successful author, even at your age, don't count yourself out of the "race" back to the moon or even better someday flying to Mars! I'd love to go with you when that day surely comes.

Ali, as you grow older you will realize how important what you learn as a child is to your future—and you will find that you never stop learning.

In reflecting back on my life as I have done in detail these past two years in the writing of my memoirs, I continue to come back to the influence my father had on me and on my life. Without knowing it at the time, he not only gave me the tools but the values and the understanding of commitment needed to face my challenging future.

He would always impress upon me "that if it's worth doing, it was worth doing right the first time, because you might not get another chance." But he never asked for more than my best—whether in the classroom, athletic field, or wherever—but always reminded me that I was the only person who knew what my best really was.

Perhaps his confidence in me, his guidance and love, along with his pride and encouragement gave me whatever it was that allowed me to reach for the stars.

Let me add what I've learned since—nothing is impossible—if I can go to the moon before you were born, then there is nothing you cannot do in your lifetime, if you allow yourself to dream and then make a commitment to seeing your dreams become reality.

Ali, I hope with this letter others are encouraged to reach for their own star. They might be surprised with the results! See you on Mars.

Sincerely,

Eugene A. Cernan

May 20, 2000

Dear President Faulkner:

My parents went to the University of Texas at Austin and my brother is a sophomore. We are a Longhorn family! Even though I am only thirteen years old, I am writing to you with a special request.

I will soon be an author and hope you will help me accomplish my goal. My book, which is just for kids, is all about saying 'thank you' and will come out in the spring of 2001. It will be jam-packed with creative thank-you letters to inspire other kids to write. I have also written famous people and asked them the importance of saying thank you.

Here's how you can help me. I hope you will send me a letter that tells kids why saying thank you is so important *even when they go off to college*. Any words of encouragement that you can share with kids will really be meaningful. I hope you will help me out and write me back. Remember that kids will be reading it and you just might help make the world a more thoughtful place!

Being an author is not an easy job, especially when you are only thirteen. I promise to do a great job, inspire a more thoughtful world, and will send you a copy! I have included a permission form and hope to hear from you soon.

With many thanks,

Ali Spizman

13 years old

OFFICE OF THE PRESIDENT

THE UNIVERSITY OF TEXAS AT AUSTIN

Dear Ali:

Thank you for inviting me to contribute to your book.
See how easy it is to say thank you?
As president of the largest university in the country—nearly 50,000
students!—I am called upon to deliver several speeches a week, and
often as many as three in one day. I usually begin each speech by thanking the person or group that has invited me. I congratulate alumni,
acknowledge their achievements, and thank them for their public service
and exemplary lives. I thank students for choosing The University of
Texas at Austin. I thank their parents for sending them to this special
place. I thank professors for being outstanding teachers and staff members for their contributions to this grand enterprise. Thanking people is a
big part of my job.

In spite of its size, I have found that The University of Texas is a
polite, congenial community. People here still believe in manners.
Students say "No, sir," and "Yes, ma'am" and "Thank you, sir." Texas
hospitality is alive and well—and it is genuine. These small courtesies
make life more friendly and enjoyable for everyone.

Letters are an especially effective way to express gratitude. The writer
of a "thank you" letter sends a gift that is always welcome.

Thank you, Ali, for asking me to share my thoughts with you and others. Good luck with your book and in all your future endeavors. And
when it comes time for you to choose a college, please consider The
University of Texas at Austin, where we have one of the nation's leading
writing programs at our James A. Michener Center for Writers. I am
impressed by your initiative, ingenuity, and thoughtfulness.

Sincerely,

Larry. R. Faulkner
President

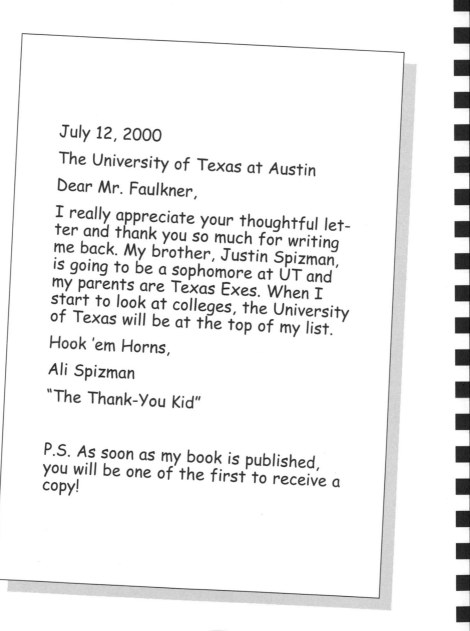

July 12, 2000

The University of Texas at Austin

Dear Mr. Faulkner,

I really appreciate your thoughtful letter and thank you so much for writing me back. My brother, Justin Spizman, is going to be a sophomore at UT and my parents are Texas Exes. When I start to look at colleges, the University of Texas will be at the top of my list.

Hook 'em Horns,

Ali Spizman

"The Thank-You Kid"

P.S. As soon as my book is published, you will be one of the first to receive a copy!

Dear Governor Roy Barnes:

I am soon to be a published author, and hope you will help me in a very special way that will inspire thousands of kids. My mom is also an author and her books are right there in your library! I hope to make a difference like she has and need your assistance.

My name is Ali Spizman and I am only thirteen years old. I have already been a kid's reporter on national television and am now writing a book. I hope to do something positive to help other kids, and decided if I wrote a book it would be a great way to share my ideas.

I am currently writing a children's book which is going to be published by Longstreet Press (March 2001). My book will encourage kids to say thank you! I would like to request a special favor from you. Would you please consider sending me a letter that shares your feelings about why saying thank you is so important?

I would like to include your letter in my book and sincerely appreciate the time you will take to write me. Thank you so much for your time! I am so proud of your accomplishments and hope you will write me back soon. Keep up the great work!

With lots of smiles,

Ali Spizman

STATE OF GEORGIA
OFFICE OF THE GOVERNOR
ATLANTA 30334-0900

Dear Ali:

Thank you for your recent note to me announcing that you are soon to be a published author at the age of thirteen! I am honored that you have asked me to contribute my thoughts on the importance of saying "thank you."

The people of the South are remarkable for their graciousness. From the cradle young children are drilled daily to "tell Aunt Susie thank you," in the hopes of raising a polite and socially acceptable child. If these caring and strict lessons are missed in childhood, then the child can grow into a boorish and rude adult. Common courtesy is in short supply today in our busy world.

Ali, my advice to you and your peers is to learn to recognize and appreciate kindness. You can avoid frustration in business and life by remembering just two words: thank you. It is said that anyone too busy to say "thank you" will get fewer and fewer chances to say it.

I commend you for your efforts, encourage you to continue to pursue your dreams, and wish you the very best that life has to offer!

Sincerely,

Roy E. Barnes

Roy E. Barnes

Chapter Nine

Thank-You Poems

When saying thank you, it is really fun to express your thanks in the form of a poem. Poems are something that everyone saves throughout time, so take your time and try to be clever. My grandpa, whom we call "Honey," and my Grandma Phyllis saved the poems my mom wrote when she was a little girl. They also saved the cards she created and made just for them.

Even if you aren't great at rhyming, it's easy to learn how to make a rhyme every time. I love to rhyme words, but I also find a rhyming dictionary to be help-ful to have on hand. Here's a quick trick that helps me when writing a poem. Whenever I need to rhyme a word, all I do is go through the alphabet and think of a word that rhymes for each letter. If I want to rhyme the word "bright," I start with A and end with Z and think of all the possible words to use. For example, bright rhymes with height, kite, light, might, night, right, sight, and tight.

I hope the following poems will inspire you to be creative. Once you get the hang of it, it's easy and you'll be able to write a poem in no time at all!

A Family Prize

When it comes to family,
How can I thank you guys?
Because you are so special,
Our blue-ribbon prize.

I am the winner,
I am feeling elated.
I am the luckiest kid
Because we are related.

A GRAND THANK-YOU

Whenever I'm with you,
You make me giggle.
And whenever you tickle me,
You make me wiggle.

You make me smile
When we are together.
You are the greatest grandparents,
I will love you forever.

MY THOUGHTFUL FRIEND

I have a friend
Who's so sweet to me.
The most thoughtful friend
There could ever be.

You'll be with me
Wherever I go.
You're the kindest friend
I'll ever know.

THANK YOU, FRIENDS

I am thankful for many friends you see,
They would fill the alphabet from A to Z.
Abbie, Amy, Aubrey, Gabrielle, Laura,
Nicole, Romy, Stephanie, Tanya, and more,
Plus loads of others whom I adore.

Too many to mention
Too much to say,
My friends, I thank you
In a million ways!

THANK YOU, MOM

You're a cooking pro,
You're the carpool queen.
You're the sweetest mom
I've ever seen.

You cheer me up
When I'm feeling blue.
I count my blessings
Because of you!

WORLD'S BEST DAD

If I traveled the world,
I could never find
A dad like you,
Who's always so kind.

You're smart, you're bright,
You're always so wise.
When I'm having fun with you,
Time always flies.

To My Brother

Thank you, Brother,
For always being there.
For being nice to me,
And not pulling my hair.

I know we bicker,
But that will pass.
I'll keep you as my brother,
Because at least you have class.

Thanks to You

A thank-you
Is the very best way
To express my feelings
Every day.

A thank-you
For all you do,
Because I really
Appreciate you!

A Great Big Thank-You!

A thank-you
Is a special thing.
You can write it with a pen,
Or give it with a rrrrr-ing.

It's quick and easy
And simple to do,
And there will always be dozens
Reserved just for you.

Thank You, Teacher

A thank-you for my teacher
Would never be enough,
To thank you for your hard work
And teaching us lots of stuff.

Your students think you're awesome,
You're one of a very special kind.
So thank you, our dear teacher,
For enlightening all our minds.

A THANK-YOU A DAY

Teacher, teacher,
What do we say?
A thank-you for our teacher
Each and every day.

You care, you are kind,
You are always so sweet.
You are a wonderful teacher
We think you are neat!

THANK YOU FOR THE INVITATION

I'm delighted,
excited,
you invited me.
To a very cool
party at which
everyone we'll see.
Thank you so much
for your invitation.
I'm looking forward
to your special celebration!

A GREAT BIG THANK-YOU

A thank-you is a tiny thing
No larger than a minute,
But it's filled with all my love
And a great big thanks is in it!

Thank You for Your Hospitality

You rolled out the red carpet
And everyone will agree:
You treat your guests
Like royalty!

Chapter Ten

Spreading Thank-You Kindness

I'll never forget the Thanksgiving Day we celebrated in honor of the turning of the century. It was Thanksgiving Day 1999, and my mom and I decided to do a good deed for someone else to express our thanks. We filled a shopping bag with toys and a beautiful doll and took them to a nearby children's hospital in Atlanta, right before our family Thanksgiving dinner.

We left the toys at the front desk with a nurse who reassured me there were many children who would really appreciate these toys.

As I looked around the room, I saw so many sick children and even a little girl in a wheelchair. I knew our visit was important and this was the real meaning of "giving thanks."

Every day can be a day you give thanks. In fact, saying thank you is a way to count your blessings in life. From thank-you notes to doing good deeds, there are many ways to express your feelings. I call this "spreading thank-you kindness." Sometimes it's seeing your parent unload the groceries and offering to help, while other times it's doing a good deed for someone you don't even know.

We all have a great opportunity to make the world a happier place, and all you have to do is take a little bit of time daily to make someone else smile or feel better. This chapter will share ideas you can do in the spirit of spreading thank-you kindness. I'm sure you have many ideas of your own, and I hope you will join me in making the world a very kind place.

DO SOMETHING NICE FOR SOMEONE YOU DONT KNOW: Whether it's unloading groceries or holding a door, doing a good deed for someone else can make a difference. When you are in line at the grocery checkout, consider helping the person behind you unload their basket, too. This is especially nice when it's an elderly person. It makes the other person feel good, and it will make you feel good, too.

CELEBRATE YOUR BIRTHDAY WITH A GOOD DEED: Every birthday I like to do something for someone else, and there are many things you can do. Bring toys or bake cookies for the children at a homeless shelter. Or save your allowance and make a contribution to a good cause. Consider creating a tradition in celebration of your special day, and do something meaningful for someone who is less fortunate. You can brighten someone else's life on your happy day.

BE A GOOD NEIGHBOR: If your neighbor has a dog, they would probably love to have someone come play with it sometimes. Ask permission and see if you can walk their dog next time you go for a walk. It's fun, plus you'll enjoy the company of a new four-legged friend.

WHO'S THE BOSS?: When someone goes out of their way at a store or a place of business, think about what a great deed you can do by writing their boss. Ask them for their boss's name and address, and share your feelings about what a great employee the boss has and how smart the boss was to hire him or her. If you are at a store and someone is really terrific, ask to see the manager and brag about this employee.

DONATE A BOOK: Books are a wonderful way to say thank you or to give someone a lasting gift. After you finish reading a book you could donate it to a library, children's hospital, or even a homeless shelter so every kid could expand their reading. Just think of your favorite book and how much you enjoyed reading it. Pass on the good deed and share a good book.

CLEAN OUT YOUR CLOSET: Sometimes one person's trash is another person's treasure. I'm not talking about your worn-out sneakers, but you just might have some clothes you have outgrown and things you don't want anymore that would mean the world to someone else less fortunate. There are many organizations you can donate these items to, so clean out your closet often and do a good deed.

HAVE A HEART: Generosity is a way of life. It's like a kite that sails around the air and enjoys itself. Being generous might mean welcoming a new kid to your class, or spreading your kindness in quiet ways, like cheering someone up when they are feeling blue. Or calling a friend when she is sick to make sure that she has her homework. And also helping someone learn something new. Every day you have a chance to do something good, but it takes a person with a big heart to just do it.

MAKE A THANK-YOU KIT FOR SOMEONE: Tell a friend she is the ultimate thank-you person! Fill a container or envelope with stamps, thank-you cards, personalized notes, and return labels that you make on the computer. This is a fun way to say thank you, and you're bound to get a thank-you right back.

READY, SET, RECYCLE: Recycling is a way to thank the earth. By doing so, you will make a difference for future generations. Also, don't litter and pollute Mother Nature. There are many ways to help keep the environment clean, and we can all pitch in.

GIVE A COMPLIMENT: Words are free and fabulous and can be a great way to say thank you. Make someone feel great by telling them something they have done well that has helped you. From a teacher to just a pal of yours, be specific and tell them what they did that you appreciate.

THEYLL EAT YOUR WORDS UP: Waitresses and waiters work hard when they are trying to get you and loads of other people their food. Don't forget to say thank you and tell the manager of the restaurant what a super job they did waiting on you.

REMEMBER REMINDER: Everyone forgets things now and then, and this is one thank-you that will be appreciated. Remind a friend or family member when it's someone else's birthday, anniversary, or special occasion. Helping others to be thoughtful is an easy thing to do.

DADDY-O VIDEO: We all have favorite celebrities and television shows. Call a friend or relative when a show comes on that you know they'll really enjoy. You could also set the VCR and tape a show that your favorite person loves but will miss because they aren't home or are out of town. When I tape a show for my dad, I call it a DADDY-O VIDEO.

SAY CHEESE!: I love to take pictures and give them as thank-you gifts. This is a nice thing to do when someone takes you out to dinner or comes to your birthday party. You can also take a picture of you opening their gift and send the photo with your thank-you note. You'll definitely get your point across.

PLAY CARDS: Playing cards is a way to pass the time, but it's also a fun thank-you activity. Giving the gift of your time is a considerate thank-you. For example, ask your grandparents what their favorite card games are and ask them to teach you how to play a new one. The time you spend together will be something you both enjoy.

LIST IT!: Here's a great idea. When thanking someone special, make a list of all the ways you appreciate him. If your friend is turning fifteen, create a list of fifteen things you really value about him. Or, if someone is having a big birthday or anniversary, make your thank-you list reflect the number of years they are celebrating.

PARTY-TIME SURPRISE: Fill a bag with all the supplies to celebrate a party, from noise blowers to party hats and favors. Bring the bag to someone on her birthday and thank that friend or family member for making life "one big party."

PLANT A THANK-YOU: I once helped clean up the yard of an elderly woman who was too ill to do it. Her front yard was a mess, and she had no one to help her. My family volunteered to help and we spent all day bagging up the leaves and clearing the ground of sticks and trash. We also repotted her front planters, and she couldn't believe her eyes when she saw her new front yard. She was so happy and it did our hearts good.

HALF-TIME FUN: I think it's fun to remember someone's half birthday. Bake cookies or give that person a little gift that celebrates "halfway there" to their next birthday mark. It's a special way to thank someone you care about. Add a card that reads, "Happy half birthday to a full-time friend!"

CREATE A CALENDAR: Create a "Thank You" calendar and just watch all the thanks you receive from your family! Purchase a blank calendar and fill in each friend and family member's special dates, with tips about what he or she likes to do, a photo, favorite candy, etc. This will become a special way to remember everyone's birthdays and serve as a life-long record of who's who in your thank-you life.

TAPE IT: This thank-you gift is meaningful to small children. Make a copy of a tape for someone else, or even tape record yourself reading a favorite nursery rhyme or book on tape and add lots of expression. Little kids love to listen to books on tape, so this is the perfect thank-you for a kid sister or brother. Plus, now that you know how to use a tape recorder, tape a thank-you for someone you care about and involve your entire family.

A "COOL" THANK-YOU: Anyone can be a pro at making an ice-cold drink. Make a tall glass of lemonade or iced tea for someone when they are working hard or out in the hot sun. A cold drink on a hot day is a totally "cool" way to thank someone you care about.

A BLOOMING THANK-YOU: Create a set of thank-you cards for someone you wish to givej a special gift. Glue a bag of flower seeds onto a greeting card or a piece of sturdy paper folded over into a note. Just "can't wait" to say thanks? Choose impatiens flower seeds. Or, how about sunflower seed packages for someone who has really "brightened your day"? They'll love these thank-you notes, and this is one gift that will continue to spread kindness. Your thank-you will be planted in their minds forever!

Chapter Eleven

Thank-Yous You Can Gobble Up

One of the things I love doing most is baking a cake for someone special. Sounds easy, and it is! All I do is purchase a cake mix at the grocery and in an hour, I have a gift that everyone brags about. When I first starting baking cakes, my mom watched every move I made. Now I am a pro at it and am very careful. Depending on how old you are, you should always have assistance in the kitchen. Once you're my age, you'll find baking is a terrific way to say thank you and get your point across.

The following ideas are some fun ways you can give edible gifts that are incredible. Most people have a sweet tooth, but it's important to match up someone's favorite flavors with your thank-you gift. With a little research, you'll be giving thank-yous that rock!

TO THE SWEETEST PERSON ON EARTH:

Here's a quick thank-you that will get your point across. Tell someone they are really sweet with brownies, candy, or anything extra delicious. Or, fill a recloseable bag with Sweet Tarts or M&Ms and add a note: "Thank you to the sweetest person on earth!"

YOU TAKE THE CAKE:

There are all types of cakes you can bake, from chocolate to lemon to angel food. I am a master at bundt cakes, and everyone compliments me on them. Once your cake is cooled, wrap it up in a colorful plastic wrap. Add a sticker or a card that says, "Thank you for being such a good friend. You take the cake!" Or, "Being friends with you is the icing on the cake." Buy an angel food cake and thank someone special for being "an angel of a friend."

"MINT" FOR EACH OTHER:

Purchase a colorful bag and fill it with mints of every description. Tell your favorite friend, "We were 'mint' to be friends." They will love this gift and enjoy it mint by mint.

YOU'RE A LIFESAVER!:

Unwrapped Lifesavers candies can be easily strung onto a ribbon and given as a fun present, an edible necklace!

◎ I'M NUTS ABOUT YOU!

Fill up a jar with an assortment of nuts, from cashews to pecans. Make sure there are no shells and add a note that says, "I'm nuts about you!"

◎ YOU'RE A SMART COOKIE!

Give a box of cookies or even bake your own specialty. Attach a greeting and inform your friend that she is the smartest cookie you know!

◎ LET'S STICK TOGETHER:

Thank your friend with an assortment of different kinds of gum, from peppermint to watermelon. Attach a note to the bag that says, "I'd choose you for a friend a million times."

◎ YOU CRACK ME UP:

Crackers can be a good gift when you want to give a super snack for a super friend. When you're giving the gift, maybe you could put some of their favorite toppings on the side (for example, peanut butter, cheese, etc.).

◎ IT'S "BEAN" GREAT KNOWING YOU:

Recycle an egg carton. Decorate it from top to bottom. (Maybe even personalize it.) Put a different flavor of jellybean in each section for a very colorful gift.

"CHEWS" ME WHEN YOU NEED A FRIEND:
Fill a jar with a variety of chewy candy such as taffy or fruit chews. Here is an edible thank-you that someone special is bound to chew up!

GLAD YOU "POPPED" INTO MY LIFE:
Invite your friends over for a thank-you popcorn party. On the invitation, maybe say that you are glad that they "popped" into your life. Tell them that they are cordially invited to "pop right over" and attend a party "popping with fun." You can have fun making the popcorn and stringing it to make edible garlands or jewelry. Butter your friends up and let each one know that they are extra special.

YOU'RE THE WORLD'S BEST POP!:
Surprise a "pop" you love, from a grandfather to a dad, with a carton of his favorite soda. Place a sticker on the carton saying "To my favorite pop!"

YOU BRIGHTEN MY WORLD:
Make a rainbow jar by recycling any clear, cylinder-shaped jar. Choose candy in the colors of the rainbow. The first color to place is red and then orange, yellow, blue, green, indigo, violet. This gift is certain to brighten anyone's day, and it is a way to say a colorful thank-you.

THERE IS "KNOT" A FRIEND LIKE YOU:
Say thank you with anything edible that contains a knot. Pretzels are a perfect example that will get your point across in a crunchy way.

 "ORANGE" YOU GLAD WE'RE FRIENDS?:
One of my favorite things to do is to write a message with a permanent marker on a piece of fruit that has a peel. It is a creative way to say a juicy thank-you.

 BROWNIE POINTS:
Fill a box with brownies (home-baked are my very favorite). Thank a teacher or someone special for all they've done to help you. Be sure to express how many "brownie points" they have earned.

 YOU'RE OUT OF THIS WORLD!:
Here is a thank-you gift that is perfect for an amazing mom or grandma. Express your thank-you with a heavenly gift like an angel food cake, marshmallow cookies, or an "out-of-this-world" dessert.

Thanks to You!

Dear Reader,

I hope that you have enjoyed reading my book. If you choose to write a thank-you note, spread kindness, or say thank you whenever you get a chance, then I know I have accomplished my goal. Consider all the opportunities you have every day to brighten someone's life, or put a big smile on their face. Besides making them happy, you will make yourself feel happy, too! ❀ I'd love to hear how your thank-yous have made a difference. Check out my Web site at <u>www.thankyoukids.com</u>, and I look forward to hearing from you soon. ❀ With a world of thanks for joining me in my thank-you mission,

ALI SPIZMAN